From Stress to Serene:

Create your path to happiness in under an hour

– RAVI VERDI –

An environmentally friendly book printed and bound in England by www.printondemand-worldwide.com

Mixed Sources
Product group from well-managed forests, and other controlled sources
www.fsc.org Cert no. TT-COC-002641
© 1996 Forest Stewardship Council

PEFC Certified
This product is from sustainably managed forests and controlled sources
www.pefc.org

This book is made entirely of chain-of-custody materials

www.fast-print.net/store.php

From Stress to Serene

ISBN 978-178035-451-4

First published 2012 by
FASTPRINT PUBLISHING
Peterborough, England.
Printed by Printondemand-Worldwide

To my special family and all my readers, wishing you every happiness and fulfilment.

ACKNOWLEDGEMENTS

During the process of writing this workbook so many people have supported and helped me along the way. I would like to say "thank you" to:

My husband who is also my best friend, for always being there and believing in everything I do. Without you this workbook would not have been possible. I am grateful to have you in my life.

My family, particularly my parents and friends, who have always believed in all my ventures and have given me their encouragement.

The Coaching Academy for introducing me to amazing people and training me to become an incredible coach.

To Pam Lidford, who inspired and encouraged me to write this workbook and gave me the necessary self-belief.

To my editor, who has done fantastic job.

To the inspiring teachers: Anthony Robbins, Steven Covey, Deepak Chopra, Paul McKenna, Richard Bandler and Michael Neil who have helped me with their knowledge and enlightenment.

Last but not least, I would like to say a big thank you to you my readers. I hope this workbook gives you the tools to support you on your path to happiness. All the best.

CONTENTS

WHAT OTHERS SAY AFTER READING THE FIRST EDITION

"This workbook has helped me along the path to everyday positivity and decreased stress levels in an increasingly stressful world. The fabulous and easy to use techniques are effective, quick, and are accessible to everyone. Using this workbook will be an hour well spent bringing health benefits, success and happiness."

R Phull
Teacher

"As an experienced performer, I can say without hesitation that I wish I'd had Ravi's gem of a workbook at the start of my career. The stresses of both performing and trying to eke out a living in the creative arts would certainly have been transformed had I had any of Ravi's brilliant and effective exercises available to me.

The real value of what Ravi has created is that she has digested some very complex techniques into exercises that are easy to do and whose simplicity is a great gift. Their impact will be profound to anyone who is willing to commit to doing them regularly."

G Hardwick
Performance Poet & Creative Synergy Expert

"Being a student there is this constant stress which one gets not only from exams, but from doing extra-curricular activities, and writing university applications. This workbook offers simple exercises and techniques, to deal with strenuous events and with the reflective nature of the workbook, it builds one's character so that one is able deal with future stress problems. The workbook offers great joy, happiness and good living, and that's outstanding considering it took me an hour to read."

A Sami
'A'level Student

"As a GP I am more than aware that stress is a cause of many illnesses - some very serious. This workbook will help people to change their thoughts and perspectives to manage their stress levels, thus leading to healthier lifestyles. The techniques in this workbook are quick, simple and easy to apply. I recommend it."

J Alder
Doctor

"This workbook will bring both hope and practical help to anyone who finds it difficult to deal with strenuous situations in everyday life.
I found the techniques and exercises extremely useful giving compelling results. Being a mother and working fulltime in investment banking has been extremely challenging for me and this workbook just made my life simpler.
Thank you Ravi for producing a quick and easy read that is affordable and light to carry in your handbag".

M Channa
Mother / Investment banking professional

"Stress is a sensitive, difficult subject to grapple for most individual until you read Ravi's workbook. The simplicity of this workbook makes it fully impacting and filled with useful exercises that are easy adopt in everyday life. This workbook is a 'must have' for anyone keen to effectively manage their stress."

S Atanda
HR Consultant – ARS Group

INTRODUCTION

Have you ever felt stressed out?

Would you like to feel good and be relaxed instead of being stressed?

Have you ever felt that now is the time to take control of your life?

In your hand, you hold a workbook to help you **relax** and **de-stress** by providing you with **simple** and **powerful** techniques to reduce stress in any aspect of your life. It will give a valuable overview on how to manage your everyday stress.

When you begin using these techniques on a regular basis, you will **increase** your **energy** levels and find you become more **efficient** and **effective** at handling stressful situations or events or problems. Most importantly, they will make you **feel good** and help you to create your path to happiness.

Everybody has some kind of stress. However, not everyone has the **techniques** to deal with it.

Quite often when people are stressed they tend to take time out, go on holiday, go out with friends, buy new clothes, listen to music, exercise etc. This only makes them feel good for a short time, whereas my clients say they receive lasting benefits.

For you to get the same lasting benefits, you must start to become aware of your **thoughts**, your **feelings** and your **language**.

This workbook is divided into three parts:

Part 1: All about stress

Part 2: Techniques to manage your stress and become relaxed

Part 3: Daily techniques to help you feel good

Throughout the workbook you will see this sign. An exercise will follow. For you to get the best results, please complete the exercise before moving on.

Remember, one small change could have a huge impact on your life. Make a decision today to select one of the techniques I will be sharing in this workbook and commit to practising it for a month. You will notice a true difference in how you manage your stress.

I am sure you will find these techniques useful and I wish you great success in creating your path to happiness. I look forward to hearing how you get on. You can contact me through my website: www.raviverdi.com

Ravi Verdi

PART 1

ALL ABOUT STRESS

"If you ask what is the single most important key to longevity, I would have to say it is avoiding worry, stress and tension. And if you didn't ask me, I'd still have to say it."

George Burns

WHAT IS STRESS?

Everybody's definition of stress is different.

What does the word stress mean to you?

The dictionary definition of stress is:
"The body's reaction to change that requires physical, emotional or mental adjustment."

When a stressful situation/event/problem occurs our body's fight/flight response becomes activated. When this happens our body releases a range of stress hormones such as adrenaline, noradrenalin and cortisol.

The fight/flight response is there to prepare the body to protect itself from perceived attacks and harm. As a result, when it kicks in, your immune system is suppressed and your heart rate increases along with your breathing rate. You may also sweat, experience butterflies in your stomach and find your muscles becoming tense. These physical responses create all the symptoms of stress e.g. worry, anxiety etc.

Our body goes back to normal when the threat is removed and the hormones: adrenaline, noradrenaline and cortisol return to their usual levels.

THE DIFFERENT TYPES OF STRESS

Survival stress:
This happens when you have a burst of energy to protect yourself in a life-threatening situation. An example of this is when you find yourself running away from imminent danger, such as being chased by an angry dog.

Internal stress:
This happens when you worry about things that you have no control over. For example, some people look for situations/events/problems in order to feel stressed, even though the situations are not actually stressful.

Environmental stress:
This is the response to things around you such as noise, crowds, or perhaps pressure from work and family.

Fatigue and overworked stress:
This kind of stress builds up over time and takes a hard toll on your body, caused by over working. It can also be caused by not knowing how to manage your time well or being unable to take time out and relax.

What type of stress do you have?

WHAT HAPPENS WHEN YOU GET STRESSED?

Signs of stress are recognised under three categories: **physical, emotional** and **behavioural**.

Below is a list of the most common sign:

Physical	Emotional	Behavioural
Aches & pains	Anger	Accident prone
Breathlessness	Anxiety & nervousness	Increased alcohol intake
Palpitations	Increased worrying	Drug dependence
Skin irritation	Lacking confidence	Forgetting things
Allergies	Feeling tense	Inability to relax
Nausea	Day dreaming	Tiredness
Weight gain/loss	Guilt	Irritability
Muscle twitching	Helplessness	Loss of interest in sex
Menstrual changes	Lack of concentration	Overeating
Recurring illness	Lack of self esteem	Loss of appetite
Colds & coughs	Mood swings	Self neglect
Diarrhea	Blame & arguing	Sleep problems
Fainting	Feeling out of control	Impaired speech
Tightness in chest	Weepiness	Poor time management

What are your signs of stress in each category?

STRESS AFFECTS YOUR PERFORMANCE

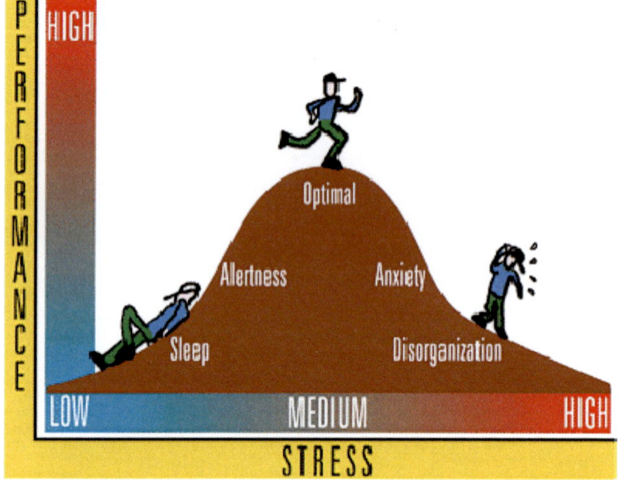

Yerkes Dodson Law 1908; Stress vs. Performance

The diagram above illustrates 3 key points:

1. Low stress levels cause your performance to drop, therefore, it is important to have some stress.

2. Medium stress increases your performance levels, therefore, it is all about knowing how to manage your stress.

3. High stress levels cause your performance to drop, therefore, it is important to learn how to reduce your stress to manageable levels.

WHAT IS STRESSING YOU OUT?

Before you read any further, take a moment to make a list of the things that are causing you stress:

1.

2.

3.

4.

5.

6.

7.

8.

9.

10.

11.

12.

13.

*Select two stressful events from your list, to which you want a solution. Write the chosen events in the format below. You will use these examples in Part 2 to find solutions to these situations/problems/events. Begin with **A** then **B** and then **C**.*

A -Activating event that is stressing you *This is the event /situation/problem that triggered your thoughts and feeling.*	**B –Beliefs/ thoughts** *These are the thoughts/beliefs went through your head when the event occurred.*	**C -Consequences** *These are your feelings, experiences and the actions you took.*
Example Preparing for a presentation **On a scale of 1-10 how stressed are you about this (1 not stressed 10 very stressed): e.g.** 8	***Thoughts:*** My audience may not like my style of presenting, is there any point in me doing it? **Beliefs:** I am not a good presenter, there are others who are better than me.	***Feelings:*** Worried, anxious & nervous ***Actions:*** Can't practise doing the presentation. Calling the organisers to cancel.

PART 2

TECHNIQUES TO MANAGE YOUR STRESS AND BECOME RELAXED

"The person with the most flexible behaviour will control the outcome of a situation."
NLP presupposition

BE RESOURCEFUL

In order for you to get the best results it is vitally important that you do the following:

- Change your state to be positive
- Manage your breathing pattern(s)
- Create a feel good anchor

By doing these three things, you will become more resourceful at solving your stress. If you do not, you will be just wasting your time!

"Adopting the right attitude can convert a negative stress into a positive one."
Hans Selye

MANAGING YOUR STATE

Be in a good state of mind! Think about how you manage yourself in terms of your feelings and your thoughts.

Did you know that throughout the day your state changes many times, due to the situations/events/ problems you may encounter and the people you interact with?

Sometimes you may not be aware of this happening.

Think what happens when you meet people you do not get on well with?
How do your physiology, tone of voice and your behaviour change?

Think what happens when you meet people you do get on well with?
How do your physiology, tone of voice and your behaviour change?

Having thought about the above exercise, you will now be more aware of how your state changes. The great thing is when you become aware of your state, you will have the ability to change and choose the state you want, in any given situation.

How can you use this to manage your state with someone who you may not get on with?

The diagram below shows how what you do, feel and think are linked in a cycle of continuation.

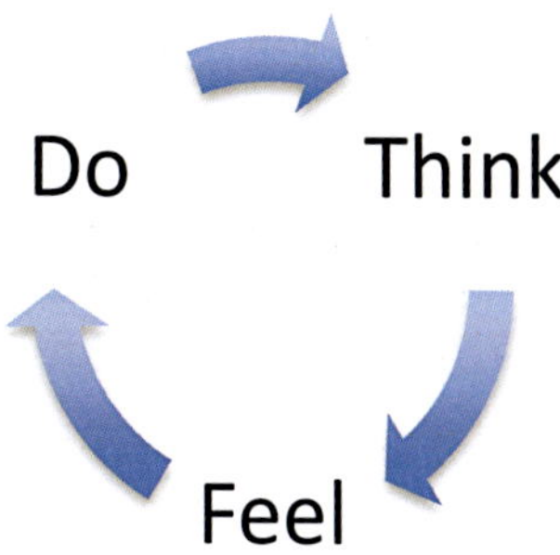

This means if you are thinking negative thoughts you will have negative feelings and therefore, the actions you take will be negative as a result of those thoughts and feelings. Consequently, this becomes a vicious cycle, which drags you down.

Remember, negative thoughts are much stronger than positive ones and can have a hugely negative impact on you.

On the other hand, if you think positively, you feel good and have a positive state of mind. This is the best situation by far.

Try this exercise:

Think of a time when you felt low and then answer the following questions:

1. How did it feel to be in a low state?
2. What did that do for you?
3. What did you notice about yourself while in this state?
4. Where were you looking, what were you thinking?
5. How were you standing or sitting?
6. What was your energy level like?
7. What were your expectations while in this state?
8. How easy is it to stay in this state?
9. What are the benefits of staying in this state?

This time do the same exercise while being in a good state.

Think of a time when you felt good and answer the following questions:

1. How did it feel to be in a good state?
2. What did that do for you?
3. What did you notice about yourself while in this state?
4. Where were you looking, what were you thinking?
5. How were you standing or sitting?
6. What was your energy level like?
7. What were your expectations while in this state?
8. How easy is it to stay in this state?
9. What are the benefits of staying in this state?

Now compare your answers. What have you learnt from this exercise?

In future, how will you remember to be aware of your state?

By being aware of this information, how can you use it to your advantage?

BREATHING PATTERNS

When you are stressed out, your breathing patterns change. The symptoms you start to experience are: shallow breathing, anxiety, chronic fears and emotions, attention problems, inability to relax, fatigue and depression.
Managing your breathing pattern is important when feeling stressed. Sadly, all too often our bodies take control of our breathing without us even being aware of it. However, when you feel stressed out it is important to breathe in a particular way.

Below are two different breathing exercises, both of which will help you to relax and feel calm quickly.

Breathing work 1

This exercise can be done whilst sitting down, standing or walking.
Place you hands on your stomach and breathe in through your nose for a count of 5, whilst breathing in you should feel your stomach muscles push out.

Now breathe out through the mouth for a count of 10, still keeping your hands on your stomach and feeling your stomach muscles pushing in.

Repeat this 15 times.
This will allow you to breathe more deeply, as it is a more natural and relaxed way.

Breathing work 2

This exercise is to be done whilst standing.

Place your hands on your hipbones with thumbs pointing out over the kidney area and your fingers either side of the stomach.

Breathe out fully through your mouth, then squeeze your hands gently, resisting breathing in through your nose. Let go and breathe normally. Repeat this 10-15 times.

This breathing exercise is great to use when feeling anxious.

DID YOU KNOW?

Early Yogis, Tibetan Masters and Shamanic Healers around the globe all say the following, "Perfect Breath, Perfect Health.'
People with poor breathing patterns have number of health issues due to their lower oxygen levels, which occur when people do not breathe out fully, therefore not allowing the body to have the correct exchange of oxygen and carbon dioxide. These breathing exercises allow your lungs to be filled with fresh air by releasing old air. Ideally, when you breathe out, it should take twice as long as when you breathe in.

Make a commitment to yourself to do these breathing exercises every day and you will notice many benefits.

CREATE A FEEL GOOD ANCHOR

This technique will help you take control of your stress and show you how to increase the regularity and intensity of natural relaxation. It will help you develop inner calmness, allowing you to feel good as a daily part of your life.

Read through the exercise first so you know what to do.

1. Remember a time when you felt really calm, happy and in control (if you cannot remember a time, try to imagine how you would feel being calm, happy and in control in a perfect scenario.) Relive that memory as if it were happening to you right now, seeing what you saw, hearing what you heard, and feeling what you felt.

2. As you run this feeling and image of being calm, happy, and in control:

- Make the colours brighter
- The sound sharper
- The feelings stronger

3. Run through this memory several times. When you start feeling really good and relaxed, squeeze your thumb and middle finger on any hand. Whilst doing this continue to run this memory 5 more times. You will know when to stop, as you will start feeling the sensation spread through your body.

4. Walk around for 5 seconds then test the anchor by squeezing your thumb and your middle finger. Notice how much the desired feelings are felt. It is important during this test that you do not actively try to bring about the desired feelings, but rather let the anchor do its work.

5. This anchor can be used at anytime in the future to bring natural relaxation for any situation.

Think of a situation in the future when you could use this anchor?
How could you remember to trigger the anchor?
How could the situation be different?

ABC MODEL

This technique is designed to help you control your thoughts. It suggests that emotional problems do not stem directly from the problem that besets us, but from the irrational and false notions we hold about it.

Earlier you wrote down two stressful events in a particular format (see diagram below.) This was done using the ABC model, which was identified by Dr Albert Ellis, an American psychologist.

This is the ABC model technique.

A -Activating event stressing you out *This is the event /situation/problem that triggered your thoughts and feeling.*	**B –Beliefs/ thoughts** *These are the thoughts/beliefs that went through your head when the event occurred.*	**C -Consequences** *These are your feelings and the actions you took.*
Example Preparing for a presentation **On a scale of 1-10 how stressed are you about this (1 not stressed 10 very stressed): eg** 8	***Thoughts:*** My audience may not like my style of presenting, is there any point in me doing it? ***Beliefs*:** I am not a good presenter, there are others who are better than me.	***Feelings:*** Worried, anxious & nervous ***Actions:*** Can't practise doing the presentation. Calling the organisers to cancel.

Refer back to the example and notice how the activating event triggered your thoughts and beliefs, how your thoughts triggered your feelings and how your feeling caused you to take those actions.

A + B = C

Many people believe that emotional tensions are the direct result of stressful situations. However, they are unaware that our thoughts play a large role in influencing how we feel.

"Many of us do not realise that our perceptions about events or our thinking style and our attitudes can also contribute to our levels of stress."

Professor C. Cooper

Using the two examples you prepared earlier (page 14), write down the events in the same format as shown below, but this time fill in each part by referring to the points that follow:

A -Activating event stressing you out	**B –Beliefs/ thoughts**	**C -Consequences**
Answer to P1 ***Activating event:*** *Answer to P5* **On a scale of 1-10 how stressed are you about this (1 not stressed 10 very stressed):**	*Answer to P3* ***Thoughts:*** **Beliefs:**	*Answer to P2* ***Feelings:*** *Answer to P4* ***Actions:***

1. Write down the activating event.

2. Write down how you would prefer to feel instead.

3. Identify the thoughts and beliefs you would have to have to create the feelings you prefer point 2.

4. List the actions you would have to take as a result.

5. Rate your level of stress on a scale of 1-10 (1 not so stressed- 10 very stressed.)

By practising this technique you will find that it puts things into perspective and makes you evaluate your thoughts and beliefs. After completing this task, answer the following questions:

What have you learnt by completing this exercise?
How can you use this exercise in the future?
If you continue using this exercise what impact will it have on your stress levels?

"Everything can be taken from a man but one thing: the last of human freedoms to choose one's attitude in any given set of circumstances, to choose one's own way."

Viktor Frankl

EMPOWERING QUESTIONS TO SOLVE A PROBLEM

This technique is all about asking yourself empowering questions to solve an event/problem/situation. By asking the right questions you can always be in control.

What questions do you ask yourself when you are stressed?

The questions below will help you to eliminate most of your stress/worry. They do this by taking your attention away from the stressful event/problem/ situation. You will be encouraged to search for solutions.

Think of an event/situation/problem which is causing you stress and worry, then answer the following questions:

1. On a scale of 1-10 (1 not so stressed- 10 very stressed) how stressed are you about this event/problem/situation?

2. Identify three positive points about this event/problem/ situation.

3. Identify three things have you learnt from this event/problem/ situation.

4. How would you prefer the event/problem/ situation to be instead?

5. What must you stop doing in order to get the results you want?

6. What are you keen to do to get the results you desire?

7. How can you motivate yourself to take the actions required?

8. Identify three steps can you take today to get things moving in the right direction?

9. Are there any pitfalls in taking the actions? If so how will you overcome each one?

10. Having answered the questions, check on a scale of 1-10 to see how stressed you are now in comparison to your previous score (1 not stressed- 10 very stressed.)

What difference has this technique made to the event/situation/problem that is stressing you out?

WHAT THINKING ERRORS DO YOU HAVE?

There are many thinking errors we have which are also known as negative thoughts. Remember 'negative feelings and thoughts will get the better of you, they will drag you down, as negative thoughts are much stronger and lead to stress.'
Below is a list of some of the thinking errors.

All or Nothing:
This is when your thinking is black or white rather than in shades of grey. You see things in extreme terms such as good or bad, right or wrong, success or failure.
Example:
"I have got to get this 100% perfect. I always make this mistake. I'll never get the hang of it."

Labelling:
This is when you attach negative labels to yourself. Every time anything goes wrong, however small, it reinforces the label you have created.
Example:
"I'm useless. I am a failure. I am not the sort of person who can cope with all of this. I am so unlucky."

I should/ I must/ I can't:
This is when you set unrealistic standards for yourself. When you do not achieve them you end up feeling bad.
Example:
"I should be able to cope with all this work. I must do better this time. I can't handle this."

Magnification:

This involves blowing things out of proportion.

Example:

"I failed my promotion interview - my career is ruined. We didn't win the contract- it is the end of the world."

Predicting:

This is when we predict negative future outcomes.

Example:

"I am going to really embarrass myself in this meeting. If I make a mistake everyone will laugh at me. I bet everyone is thinking that I am an idiot."

Discounting:

This is when we minimise the positive factors in favour of negative aspects.

Example:

"He is only saying my work is good because he feels sorry for me. I was really lucky to make that sale. I can't believe I passed the exam – the questions must have been easy."

What thinking errors do you have which cause you stress?
Make a list of them.

Challenge each thinking error by answering the following questions:

1. What impact is this particular thinking error having on you?

2. Has anyone confirmed your thinking error? How do you know this? What evidence do you have?

3. How is this stopping you from achieving your goals?

4. What can you say instead to reverse your thinking error?

5. How will you benefit from using this new statement?

6. What difference has been made to your thinking errors now that you have challenged yourself?

CHALLENGE YOUR NEGATIVE BELIEFS

Beliefs are the thoughts and ideas that we no longer question. They shape the direction of our lives because we act as if they are true and they therefore become true for us. They may be empowering or they may be limiting.

The negative beliefs are the limiting ones and its important to be aware of them. It is imperative that you change them.

If you tell yourself regularly "I am stupid," "I will never lose weight," "I am fat," "I am unhappy" and so on, eventually this is what will happen - you will start to believe it and as a result you will start to feel low.

What negative beliefs do you hold about yourself?
For each belief ask yourself:

1. Where did this belief come from?
2. Who gave you this belief?
3. How do you feel about the person who gave you this belief?
4. What is the belief costing you on a daily basis?

5. What will holding this belief mean for you in the long term?

6. How will your life be different if you let go of this belief?

Having challenged your old beliefs, ask yourself:

7. What belief do I want instead of the old one?

8. What will the benefits be of having the new belief?

HOW TO CHANGE YOUR BAD MOODS

We all have choices on how we shape our moods and our thoughts. We all face situations that can stress us out. How great would it be if you could look at the situation in a different way and use it to your advantage?

Situations	Bad mood	Good mood
Stuck in traffic	"London traffic is terrible. Every morning I have to put up with this rubbish!"	"Oh well, at least I can enjoy listening to more music."
Diverted traffic/lost	"Now it going to take me ages, I'll get back late, won't get a chance to go out."	"I've learnt a new route I could benefit from in the future."
The weather is terrible	"Every one is looking miserable and I can't do anything or go out."	"I can have a chat with my friend."

What things put you in a bad mood?
What does that do to you?
How can you turn things around to create a good mood?
What positive impact will this have on you?

LEARNING FROM BAD SITUATIONS

In life bad things do happen and there are many ways you can view them. If you want to reduce your stress levels learn to ask yourself empowering questions that can help you develop.

Think of some bad situations that have occurred in your life.
By referring to each situation, I want you to ask yourself the following questions:

1. What did I learn from this situation?

2. How will these new lessons help me in the future?

3. What can I do differently in the future if this situation happened again?

MESSAGES FROM NEGATIVE EMOTIONS

Over the years I have learnt that negative emotions are very important. They are giving you the message that 'something needs to be changed.' I have also learnt if you do not acknowledge them they keep on appearing again and again. And the intensity of the emotion will get stronger. Therefore, we should be very grateful for these negative emotions as they help us to develop ourselves.

Below is a list of 10 negative emotions and how to identify them, according to Anthony Robbins:

Emotions	**Signals**
Uncomfortable	Impatient, distressed, rejected, embarrassed and uneasy
Fear	Scared, terrified, concerned and apprehensive
Hurt	Sense of loss
Anger	Irritation, resentful, rage, furious
Frustration	Held back & hindered
Disappointment	Things don't work well, sadness and defeated
Guilt	Feeling bad about things or emotions of regret
Feeling of inadequacy	Any emotion which makes you think you have no value or feel unworthy
Feeling of overload	Hopelessness, overwhelmed, depression
Lonely emotions	Separation, alone and loneliness

Think of an event, which is caused you to feel low?
What actually happened?
What did you do at the time?
What emotions did you experience?

Now, if I told you in the next few moments you could get out of those negative emotions, what difference could it make to you?

To get out of negative emotions:

You simply take **action** and **change** one of the following: your **perception** or your **procedure**.

Changing your perception:
To be done by changing how you look at the emotion or what you focus on.

Changing your procedure:
To be done by changing your approach or how you respond to the situation.

This table demonstatres the message that each of the 10 negative emotions is giving you, and the actions they invite you to take so as to remove their negative influence:[5]

Emotions	**Action Signals**
Uncomfortable	A feeling of unease. 1. Change your state. 2. Clarify what you want. 3. Take action in that direction.
Fear	Fear is a signal to get prepared to deal with something that is about to come. 1. If it is beyond your control, change your perception. Or 2. Let it go.
Hurt	Hurt is a signal that you have an expectation that is not being met or that you are feeling a sense of loss. 1. Evaluate whether or not there is a loss 2. Change your perception Or 3. Change your way of communicating your needs. Or 4.Change your behaviour.

Anger	Anger is a signal that you, or someone else, has violated an important rule you have in your life. 1. Clarify the rules or adjust them, as your rules may not match other people's rules, so if you do not change them you may be angry with them for the rest of you life.
Frustration	Frustration is a signal you are doing the same thing again and again and expecting a different result. 1. Change your approach to achieving your goal.
Disappointment	Disappointment is a signal that you need to realise that an expectation you had or an outcome you are going after is not going to happen. 1. Change your expectation to an appropriate outcome.
Guilt	Guilt is a signal that you violated your own standard and you must do something immediately to ensure you are not going to do so again in the future.

	1.Change your future behaviour.
Feeling of inadequacy	Inadequacy is a signal that you need to do something to get better. You do not need to be perfect though. 1. Take action e.g. start practising.
Feeling of overload	Overload is a signal to re-evaluate what is important to you in this situation. 1. Write down all the things you need to accomplish. 2. Prioritise. 3. Take the first thing on the list and do something about it.
Lonely emotions	Loneliness is a signal that you need connection with people. 1. Clarify what connection you need. 2. Change your perception.

Refer back to the emotions your experienced and identify the signal actions you need take.

PART 3

DAILY TECHNIQUES TO HELP YOU FEEL GOOD EVERY DAY

The techniques I am going to introduce to you now are to be used everyday. You need to make them a habit – like brushing your teeth morning and night.

Doing these exercises daily will immediately shift your feelings, behaviours and your thoughts. As a result, you will boost your energy levels and you will feel happy because your body will start to release endorphins, which are feel good hormones.

POWER OF SAYING WHAT YOU WANT IN LIFE

Do you often say what you do not want in life?

In life, you attract the things you think about the most. Have you noticed when you speak to the majority of people they talk about what they do not want, what they do not have in life and the things that are going wrong their life?
These are the people who keep on experiencing the same things again and again. This is why their stress levels increase.

Do you always talk about the things you do not have, the things you do not want?

Example:
I don't want to have small car.
I don't want to gain weight.
I don't want to have an admin job.
I don't want my business to fail.

If you are saying things like this then **STOP**!!!
- Say what you **WANT** in life.

Start making this change from today and note the difference it makes.

Example:

I want a big car.
I want to be slim.
I want a management job.
I want my business to be successful.

How can you ensure you get into the habit of saying what you want in life?

POWER OF THANK YOU

Do you ever say thank you for all the good in your life?

We all have good things happening in our lives. To really enhance your life you should say thank you when you wake in the morning and every night before you go sleep by reflecting back on your day.
Be thankful for the good things you get, the people you care about, and the people who make positive differences in your life.

You will find over time that by doing this you will gain inner peace and start getting more in life, which will create a path to happiness.

Start the day by saying "thank you for..........."
Every morning when you wake up spend time to say what you are thankful for.
If you like you can keep a daily gratitude journal.

Some of you may be saying, "I have nothing to be grateful for." Everyone does! It could even be as small as going to a coffee shop and reading a book.
Make a commitment to yourself. You will be amazed at the difference it will make in your life.

POWER OF VISUALISATION

Do you take time out to feel totally relaxed?

Visualisation is a way to take time out to revitalise yourself so you can feel relaxed and good within yourself.

Read through the exercise before your start doing it.

Think of a place where you can feel totally relaxed and absorbed. This could be:

- Sitting on the sofa in the evening with your favourite music playing.
- Going for a walk and enjoying the weather.
- Lying on a beach with the sun shining, listening to the waves.

Close your eyes and think of your chosen place and have a look around. See what you see, hear what you can hear, and feel what you can feel. Remain aware of the relaxed feeling in your body. Enjoy being there and feeling good. Spend a few moments at this place, letting those feelings spread all over your body.
Take all the time you need and enjoy it.

POWER OF ASKING FIVE KEY QUESTIONS

Every night before you go to bed, do you reflect on your day?

This is my favourite technique and I use it everyday. I have found it to be such a powerful way of reflecting on my day just before going to sleep. I even use the technique at the dinner table with the family, as I believe it is a great way of enhancing relationships with members of the family.

Everyday ask yourself, or people close to you, five questions:

1. What are the best things that happened to you today?
2. What have you learnt today?
3. What are you grateful for today?
4. Who are you grateful for in your life today?
5. What do you appreciate today?

POWER OF AFFIRMATIONS

Have you tried reprogramming yourself using affirmations?

An affirmation is a positive statement that you repeat to yourself at various times of the day. It helps you to develop positive self talk and can have a dramatic impact upon your behaviour and achievements. It is a very powerful self-development technique.

Affirmations have to be phrased in a special way:
Positive – Saying what you want
Personal – Start the affirmation with the words 'I am' and it should be stated in the present tense E.g. "I am a relaxed person," "I am an attractive person," "I am always eating healthily."

Write down three affirmations you want to say to yourself. Read them out five times in the morning, afternoon and evening.

For you to get the best results, first begin by imagining what you would see, hear and feel.

When you start this technique you will feed your subconscious mind with positive thoughts and words. You will start to build a **Positive Mental Attitude**.

PART 4

YOUR PERSONAL OVERVIEW

"It's amazing how one small change can have one big impact."

Steven J Sherman

YOUR OWN LEARNING

What have you learnt about yourself after completing the techniques outlined in this workbook?

Which is your favourite technique?

Which one will you start to implement immediately and practise for at least one month?

What difference could this technique make to your everyday life?

Please remember the techniques introduced in this workbook are simple but effective tools to help you help yourself manage your stress. If you require further stress management techniques, I will be delighted to assist you. You can contact me for workshops and one to one sessions by visiting: www.RaviVerdi.com

PART 5

ABOUT RAVI VERDI

"I am not what happened to me, I am what I choose to become."

Carl Jung

ABOUT RAVI VERDI

Ravi is a fully qualified coach, mentor and NLP Practitioner, who runs her own Coaching Practice. She is a very passionate, inspirational person, committed to supporting her clients to reduce stress in all aspects of their lives. She uses a combination of techniques to bring out the best in her clients and finds it amazingly rewarding to see her clients feeling empowered, energised and able to relax.

"The impact coaching has given to me has really changed aspects in my daily routine. I have more confidence in my own abilities to set goals with my coach Ravi. I made sure I was determined to achieve them as I could not have achieved them on my own before. I have seen a huge change in main areas of my life, so has my family. It has also made me realise coaching has been the best thing I have done as it has changed me so much. I am so positive and happy in my life. I have found the sessions to be enjoyable and fun. I would highly recommend Ravi to help you bring the best in yourself."
Client

Ravi has been in the health care industry for over 10 years, and seen the impact stress has on people. She was astonished to find out stress is a number one killer and that fifty per cent of people go to see a doctor for stress related issues.

Since making this discovery, Ravi has decided that her purpose in life is to make a difference to others, so they can begin to create their own path to happiness.
Ravi trained with Europe's premier providers of coaching training and found her life has changed by practising all that she has learnt. She believes you can achieve what you want in life by making small changes and taking action.

When not helping her clients to discover their path to happiness, Ravi enjoys spending time with her husband and family, going on holiday, reading personal development books and attending training programmes to further enhance her skills.

Ravi truly believes happiness begins from within.

Her two favourite quotes are:

"It is in your moment of decisions that your destiny is shaped."
Anthony Robbins

"Every day you spend without a smile, is a lost day."
Author Unknown

To learn more about Ravi Verdi's services visit her website: www.RaviVerdi.com